WOODTURNING

A SOURCE BOOK OF SHAPES

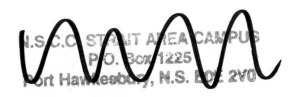

WOODTURNING

A SOURCE BOOK OF SHAPES

JOHN HUNNEX

Guild of Master Craftsman Publications Ltd

First published 1993 by
Guild of Master Craftsman Publications Ltd,
166 High Street, Lewes,
East Sussex BN7 1XU

© John Hunnex 1993

Reprinted 1994

ISBN 0 946819 45 9

Designed by Fineline Studios

Printed and bound in Singapore under the
supervision of MRM Graphics, Winslow,
Bucks, UK.

C ONTENTS

INTRODUCTION

Like a potter who works on a wheel, the woodturner on a lathe is 'limited'
to working in the round, but this is a poor description of the many shapes
that can be obtained on a lathe.

The dictionary defines shape as: 'Create, form, construct, model, fashion,
bring into desired or definite figure or form; the total effect produced by
an object's outline; shapely, well formed or proportioned, of the right or
pleasing shape.'

A 'pleasing shape' produces a warm response – a poor shape leaves us
cold. No matter how clever the technique or how beautiful the grain of the
wood, a poor shape defeats the object of the exercise.

There are a number of excellent books dealing with technique, and each
turner will adapt his or her work to suit whatever tools are available.

Lathes, tools and technique will vary from turner to turner. Setting aside
those three elements, we are left with, first, the variety of woods available,
and second, our limitless imagination!

Good technique comes with practice. With today's tools and abrasives, a
good finish can be obtained much more easily than a good shape. If you
can combine good technique with good form, your work will have a
'presence' that will please the eye. Technique should be your servant, not
your master.

Each of us experiences shape and form in a different way, and in the
contagious world of woodturning we are bound to be influenced by the
work of other turners – we should, however, always try to interpret this
influence with our personal vision.

In some of the work in this book, the wood has been covered by paint. One
of the reasons for this is to see pure shape without being distracted by
attractive grain; it is one of the quickest ways of seeing either the faults or
the merits of the turning.

These shapes are presented with the very minimum of technical detail.
Although some shapes may look similar, by looking closely you can
discover subtle differences between them.

Similar shapes can appear to be altered by the figure, grain or colour of
the wood. The wood can be light, dark, spalted, burred or sometimes
contain natural faults, but these effects should not dictate the shape of the
work. At no time should you compromise the shape because of the figuring
of the wood – the shape should be of paramount importance.

What is presented here is a selection from one man's gallery of shapes.
There are many woodturners producing wide variations of shape in both
faceplate and spindle turning, and they are all worth exploring.

TECHNICAL INFORMATION

Like many other turners, I progressed through a range of lathes, starting out with what could be afforded, and finishing up with what I wanted! I finally settled on a Harrison Graduate Short Bed Lathe, which gives me the opportunity of working from both sides of the lathe. On the inboard side I can work up to 19½in (49.6cm) wide; being right-handed, I find this a big advantage as there is no long bed in the way, and I can use longer handled tools for better control.

By removing the outside rest and using a tripod T-rest, I have the opportunity to produce larger pieces of work. A 1½hp motor has been fitted to give me the power necessary for this larger work.

There is also a removable tailstock which allows me to turn up to 15½in (39.4cm) between centres. (For longer turnings I use the Record Drillmaster which is quite adequate for my needs, as I do very little spindle turning.)

Standard gouges and scrapers are used for the majority of my work. I also use a hook tool for hollowing out around the shoulders of bottles, hollow forms etc., and have some tools that were made to enable me to reach awkward areas.

For finishing, I use a combination of power and hand sanding, using aluminium oxide cloth-backed abrasive for the latter. When the required finish has been achieved, I put on a coat of Danish Oil, buff it with a cloth, leave it for 24 hours and then repeat the process. For a higher gloss finish, I apply three coats, and for a very high polish, I use clear paste wax.

Bowls

Millions of homes throughout the world contain a mass-produced wooden bowl for domestic use. This may be one of the reasons that woodturning has become so closely associated with function rather than form.

However, with the very innovative turning that is currently taking place internationally, bowls are now becoming valued for their decorative quality. The bowls shown here can be functional or decorative or both.

When thinking about the shape of a bowl, remember that a chuck is only a holding device to allow you to turn the bowl on the lathe. It should not **dictate** the shape of the bowl. Consider reverse chucking to maintain a good flowing shape from the base.

SYCAMORE

H: 6IN (150MM)
W: 16IN (405MM)

BURR OAK

H: 8IN (200MM)
W: 17IN (432MM)

SPALTED BEECH

H: 5IN (127MM)
W:16½IN (420MM)

CEDAR

H: 5IN (127MM)
W: 13IN (330MM)

SPALTED SYCAMORE

H: 4½IN (114MM)
W: 13IN (330MM)

JARRAH

H: 4IN (100MM)
W: 13IN (330MM)

ASH

H: 7IN (178MM)
W: 17IN (432MM)

SPALTED MAPLE

H: 9IN (228MM)
W: 16IN (405MM)

Jarrah burr

H: 6in (150mm)
W: 12in (303mm)

MYRTLE

H: 6IN (150MM)
W: 15IN (381MM)

ASH

H: 8IN (200MM)
W: 17IN (432MM)

ASH

H: 10IN (253MM)
W: 9IN (228MM)

LABURNUM

H: 4IN (100MM)
W: 11IN (278MM)

SPALTED BEECH

H: 5IN (127MM)
W: 13IN (330MM)

BURR OAK

H: 8IN (200MM)
W: 14IN (355MM)

CONTAINERS

Containers, like bowls, can be functional or decorative or both.

There is a current move to use decoration on containers and other work after the turning has taken place, e.g. carving. It does mean, however, that you need to be skilful in more than one area of woodwork. Be careful with decoration, as poorly executed afterwork can ruin a good shape.

Boxes can become collectors' items, and this is an area of woodturning where turners like to demonstrate their skills. A good fit to a lid is considered to be a measure of success.

ASH

H: 8IN (200MM)
W: 5½IN (139MM)

SPALTED BEECH

H: 11IN (278MM)
W: 9½IN (240MM)

LABURNUM

H: 5½IN (139MM)
W: 5½IN (139MM)

SPALTED BEECH

H: 15½IN (392MM)
W: 7IN (178MM)

SPALTED BEECH

H: 7IN (178MM)
W: 8IN (200MM)

SONOKELING

H: 8IN (200MM)
W: 9IN (228MM)

CHERRY, COCOBOLO

H: 3IN (76MM)
W: 6IN (150MM)

ASH

H: 7IN (178MM)
W: 6IN (150MM)

RHODODENDRON

H: 8IN (200MM)
W: 7IN (178MM)

It is quite easy to imagine the plain top with some form of decoration or a change in the shape.

SPALTED BEECH

H: 8IN (200MM)
W: 5IN (127MM)

REDWOOD,
COCOBOLO

H: 7IN (178MM)
W: 5½IN (139MM)

ROPALA

H: 3½IN (88MM)
W: 4IN (100MM)

BLACKWOOD,
ROPALA INLAY

H: 2¾IN (69MM)
W: 3IN (76MM)

SONOKELING

H: 4½IN (114MM)
W: 3IN (76MM)

OLIVE TREE,
PURPLEHEART,
LABURNUM,
THUYA BURR,
SONOKELING

H: SMALLEST 2IN (50MM)
LARGEST 4½IN (114MM)
W: SMALLEST 2IN (50MM)
LARGEST 3IN (76MM)

COCOBOLO,
THUYA BURR, YEW,
ROSEWOOD

H: SMALLEST ½IN (13MM)
LARGEST 2IN (50MM)
W: SMALLEST 1⅜IN (35MM)
LARGEST 2¼IN (56MM)

Bottles

These forms are purely decorative. Some glass bottles have become design objects in their own right. They have beautiful clean lines with good shape and proportion, and are always worth looking at for these reasons alone.

Some turners hollow out from the bottom and plug the base; others like to hollow out from the top. I prefer to hollow from the top and make a close-fitting joint of the collar.

Special tools will have to be used for the hollowing out process.

You can use several species of wood for added interest. If you decide to do this, the placing of the contrasting wood becomes important as it will often appear to change the shape of the original form.

SYCAMORE

H: 6IN (150MM)
TO 8IN (200MM)
W: 6IN (150MM)
TO 8IN (200MM)

These bottles have been sprayed with matt black paint to show pure form. Spraying can show up faults in shape, as the figure of the wood can distract from pure form.

Using additional wood can appear to alter or emphasize the
shape of the work. The positioning of different wood should be
very carefully considered.

WALNUT,
PURPLEHEART, ASH

H: 8IN (200MM)
W: 7IN (178MM)

SPALTED BEECH

H: 8IN (200MM)
W: 8IN (200MM)

WALNUT ROOT,
BLACKWOOD,
PURPLEHEART

H: 6IN (150MM)
W: 6IN (150MM)

AMERICAN BLACK
WALNUT,
BLACKWOOD,
BOXWOOD

H: 6IN (150MM)
W: 5IN (127MM)

BURR ELM,
BOXWOOD

H: 5IN (127MM)
W: 5IN (127MM)

BEECH,
SPALTED BEECH,
SYCAMORE,
SPRAYED SYCAMORE

H: 6IN (150MM)
TO 8IN (200MM)
W: 6IN (150MM)
TO 8IN (200MM)

SYCAMORE,

IMBUYA

H: 8IN (200MM)
W: 5IN (127MM)

SPALTED BEECH,
IMBUYA

H: 6IN (150MM)
W: 5IN (127MM)

VARIOUS WOODS

H: 5IN (127MM)
TO 8IN (200MM)
W: 5IN (127MM)
TO 8IN (200MM)

BEECH

H: 9IN (228MM)
W: 7½IN (190MM)

BOX ELDER,
BLACKWOOD,
TULIPWOOD

H: 4½IN (114MM)
W: 5IN (127MM)

SPALTED BEECH,
BLACKWOOD,
BOXWOOD

H: 8IN (200MM)
W: 5½IN (139MM)

SPALTED BEECH

H: 6IN (150MM)
TO 9IN (228MM)
W: 5IN (127MM)
TO 7IN (178MM)

CHERRY,
RIO ROSEWOOD

H: 4½IN (114MM)
W: 4IN (100MM)

Vases

The strong influence of classic pottery shapes is clearly demonstrated in this group.

For deep cutting, I find it necessary to hold the work on a faceplate with long screws – even if this does mean losing some of the depth of the wood. This applies to both end grain and side grain: it's safer!

SPALTED BEECH

H: 6IN (150MM)
TO 9IN (228MM)
W: 5IN (127MM)
TO 6IN (150MM)

This piece of work was sandblasted; this has the effect of
wearing away the soft fibres of the wood, and leaves a very
interesting textural surface.

CEDAR

H: 8IN (200MM)
W: 8IN (200MM)

SPALTED BEECH

H: 6IN (150MM)
TO 8IN (200MM)
W: 5IN (127MM)
TO 6IN (150MM)

SYCAMORE

H: 6IN (150MM)
W: 6IN (150MM)

SPALTED BEECH

H: 9IN (228MM)
W: 5IN (127MM)

GRASS TREE ROOT

H: 7IN (178MM)
W: 6IN (150MM)

OLIVE

H: 4¾IN (120MM)
W: 3½IN (88MM)

MULBERRY

H: 8IN (200MM)
W: 7IN (178MM)

WALNUT, ASH;
BEECH, SONOKELING;
WALNUT, CHERRY

H: 6IN (150MM)
TO 9IN (228MM)
W: 3IN (76MM)
TO 4½IN (114MM)

MULBERRY

H: 6IN (150MM)
7½IN (190MM)
W: 5IN (127MM)
6IN (150MM)

CEDAR, SONOKELING

H: 9IN (228MM)
W: 8IN (200MM)

HOLLOW FORMS

Turners enjoy the challenge that these forms present. You should be prepared to lose some of your early pieces due to the degree of difficulty in hollowing them out.

Special tools have to be used.

This is one area of turning which relies heavily on the figuring of the wood, as the only function of a hollow form is that of decoration.

SYCAMORE

H: 7IN (178MM)
W: 16IN (405MM)

BURR ELM,
BOXWOOD

H: 5½IN (139MM)
W: 5½IN (139MM)

ELM

H: 3IN (76MM)
W: 8IN (200MM)

This has been sandblasted after finishing. Sandblasting only really works well on coarse-grained wood.

MAPLE,
BLACKWOOD

H: 5½IN (139MM)
W: 6IN (150MM)

SPALTED BEECH

H: 5½IN (139MM)
W: 13IN (330MM)

BURR ELM

H: 3½IN (88MM)
W: 5IN (127MM)

BURR ACACIA

H: 5IN (127MM)
W: 7½IN (190MM)

This has been sandblasted after finishing. Ash is particularly
successful with this technique.

ASH

H: 4IN (100MM)
W: 11IN (278MM)

BURR ELM

H: 4in (100mm)
W: 9in (228mm)

SPALTED BEECH

H: 10IN (253MM)
W: 7IN (178MM)

EBONY

H: 3IN (76MM)
W: 5½IN (139MM)

BUGGY RED OAK

H: 4½IN (114MM)
W: 10IN (253MM)

C LOSED FORMS

These forms introduce a little mystery to an otherwise normal bowl shape;
I often add a rim of a contrasting wood to emphasize the opening.

It is important to remember that an expanding collet chuck can determine
the size of the base of the work, which can ruin the shape if too large. If
you do use such a chuck, use it only as a holding device, then reverse the
work and make the foot complement the turning.

SPALTED BEECH,
SONOKELING

H: 5IN (127MM)
W: 11IN (278MM)

BURR ELM

H: 3IN (76MM)
W: 4½IN (114MM)

SYCAMORE

H: 4IN (100MM)
W: 11IN (278MM)

SPALTED HORNBEAM,
EBONY

H: 8IN (200MM)
W: 17IN (432MM)

BURR OAK, EBONY

H: 7IN (178MM)
W: 14IN (355MM)

The leather stitching is used as decoration. In parts of Africa today, repairing pots for dry goods is still done in this way.

JARRAH BURR

H: 4IN (100MM)
W: 5IN (127MM)

TIGER STRIPED
MYRTLE

H: 3IN (76MM)
W: 10IN (253MM)

WALNUT ROOT,
EBONY

H: 6IN (150MM)
W: 11IN (278MM)

RIPPLED ASH

H: 4IN (100MM)
W: 11IN (278MM)

SPALTED BEECH,
SONOKELING

H: 7IN (178MM)
W: 10IN (253MM)

BURR OAK, EBONY

H: 7IN (178MM)
W: 13IN (330MM)

BURR ELM

H: 3IN (76MM)
W: 10IN (253MM)

Natural Tops And Natural Edges

These forms incorporate the outer edge or bark of a tree. The natural edge
can produce an interesting silhouette to a piece of work.

On natural tops it may be useful to finish the delicate top part of the work
first, hollowing and finishing the rest of the object afterwards.

BOXWOOD

H: 3IN (76MM)
W: 4½IN (114MM)

CHERRY

H: 8IN (200MM)
W: 6IN (150MM)

BURR ELM

H: 6½IN (165MM)
W: 4IN (100MM)

LABURNUM

H: 5IN (127MM)
W: 6IN (150MM)

MULBERRY

H: 3½IN (88MM)
TO 5½IN (139MM)
W: 4½IN (114MM)
TO 5IN (127MM)

GREY GUM BURR

H: 3IN (76MM)
W: 13IN (330MM)

BURR ELM

H: 10IN (253MM)
W: 9IN (228MM)

RHODODENDRON

H: 7IN (178MM)
W: 6IN (150MM)

Jarrah burr

H: 8in (200mm)
W: 9in (228mm)

BURR ELM

H: 6IN (150MM)
W: 6IN (150MM)

LABURNUM

H: 5IN (127MM)
W: 7IN (178MM)

CHERRY, LABURNUM,
MAGNOLIA

H: 4IN (100MM)
6IN (150MM)
7IN (178MM)
W: 6IN (150MM)
5IN (127MM)
7IN (178MM)

PLATTERS AND PLAQUES

Platters hold a strong place in the history of turning, as early domestic items.

Today we often find them as decorative pieces where a craftsman can demonstrate his skill and technique. I prefer simplicity rather than decoration on my platters, and often use them as wall plaques.

Wall plaques can provide an interesting alternative to paintings, prints or photographs in room decoration.

PADAUK

W: 18IN (457MM)

ASH

W: 17IN (432MM)

ZEBRANO

W: 19½IN (495MM)

CHERRY

W: 16IN (405MM)

ELM

W: 15IN (381MM)

The piece was turned on the lathe, cut into strips on a bandsaw
and then glued together out of position.

SAPELE ON SPALTED
MAPLE

H: 11IN (278MM)
W: 6½IN (165MM)

SAPELE

H: 16IN (405MM)
W: 8IN (200MM)

The same technique was used as in the previous piece of work,
but this time it was left free standing.

The black circles were made by scorching the areas with a gas
torch after turning.

JARRAH BURR

H: 17IN (432MM)
W: 21IN (534MM)

BURR OAK

H: 16IN (405MM)
W: 26IN (660MM)

The charred effect was made using a gas torch.

BURR OAK

H: 10½IN (267MM)
W: 12½IN (318MM)

SAPELE

H: 37IN (940MM)
W: 13IN (330MM)

Variation in Shapes

The following illustrations did not fit easily into the previous categories of shapes.

Some of the shapes and effects have been obtained using tools other than the lathe, after the original turning has taken place.

ASH

H: 5IN (127MM)
W: 13IN (330MM)

This bowl was turned with a wide rim, cut into shape with a bandsaw and finished with a Powerfile and a drum sander.

LABURNUM ROOT

H: 6IN (150MM)
W: 12IN (303MM)

This was turned with an undercut rim, shaped on the bandsaw
and finished with a Powerfile and a drum sander.

ASH

H: 4IN (100MM)
W: 13IN (330MM)

After turning, the top was sculpted with a drum sander.

SPALTED BEECH

H: 10IN (253MM)
W: 12IN (303MM)

ELM

H: 16IN (405MM)
W: 6IN (150MM)

The rope handle and leather cover were added for additional
interest.

SPALTED BEECH

H: 12IN (303MM)
W: 12IN (303MM)

BURR ELM

H: 5IN (127MM)
W: 11IN (278MM)

The remaining bark on the natural edge of the wood was
scorched with a gas torch.

The bowl was turned with a wide rim, which was then cut away
with a bandsaw leaving four lugs. It was finished with a drum
sander. Holes were drilled through the lugs to allow the rope to
be threaded through.

BELI

H: 5½IN (139MM)
W: 10½IN (267MM)

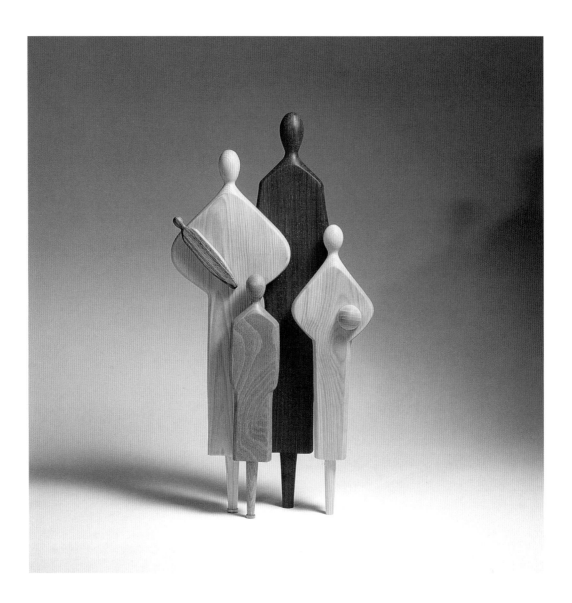

PADAUK, ASH, PINE,
WALNUT

H: 14IN (355MM)
W: 8IN (200MM)

These figures were turned between centres from a plank – they were *not* bandsawn first. The lathe was the only tool used to shape the figures, which were glued together afterwards.

I used the same technique as in the previous piece of work after seeing a group of glass bottles which reminded me of a group of people.

VARIOUS WOODS

H: 16IN (405MM)
W: 20IN (506MM)

SPALTED BEECH

H: 2IN (50MM)
W: 6½IN (165MM)

This piece of work was turned off-centre, which is good fun to do. I scorched a line with a piece of wood just inside the rim to emphasize the line.

This is the front view of the previous piece of work showing the full effect of off-centre turning.

SPALTED BEECH

H: 2IN (50MM)
W: 6½IN (165MM)

B I O G R A P H Y

John Hunnex was born in London in 1930. He moved to Kent in 1984 after retiring from Goldsmiths College where he had lectured in photography for many years.

He has been turning wood in his spare time since 1957, but after retirement has been able to devote all of his time to what he describes as his 'obsession'. He enjoys producing a wide variety of work in both native and exotic woods.

He is a founder member of the Association of Woodturners of Great Britain and is also a member of the American Association of Woodturners. He has attended woodturning seminars in the UK and the USA, and his work has been featured in the magazines *Woodworkingtoday*, *Woodworker* and *Woodturning*.

He exhibits regularly in Kent and Sussex and occasionally in other areas.

OTHER TITLES AVAILABLE FROM GMC PUBLICATIONS LTD

BOOKS

Woodworking Plans and Projects	GMC Publications
40 More Woodworking Plans and Projects	GMC Publications
Woodworking Crafts Annual	GMC Publications
Turning Miniatures in Wood	John Sainsbury
Woodcarving: A Complete Course	Ron Butterfield
Pleasure and Profit from Woodturning	Reg Sherwin
Making Unusual Miniatures	Graham Spalding
Furniture Projects for the Home	Ernest Parrott
Seat Weaving	Ricky Holdstock
Green Woodwork	Mike Abbott
The Incredible Router	Jeremy Broun
Electric Woodwork	Jeremy Broun
Woodturning: A Foundation Course	Keith Rowley
Upholstery: A Complete Course	David James
Upholstery: Techniques and Projects	David James
Making Shaker Furniture	Barry Jackson
Making Dolls' House Furniture	Patricia King
Making Tudor Dolls' Houses	Derek Rowbottom
Making Georgian Dolls' Houses	Derek Rowbottom
Making Period Dolls' House Furniture	Derek & Sheila Rowbottom
Heraldic Miniature Knights	Peter Greenhill
Furniture Projects	Rod Wales
Restoring Rocking Horses	Clive Green & Anthony Dew
Making Fine Furniture	Tom Darby
Making & Modifying Woodworking Tools	Jim Kingshott
The Workshop	Jim Kingshott
Sharpening: The Complete Guide	Jim Kingshott
Multi-centre Woodturning	Ray Hopper
Woodturning Wizardry	David Springett
Complete Woodfinishing	Ian Hosker
Making Little Boxes from Wood	John Bennett
The Complete Dolls' House Book	Jean Nisbett
Decorative Woodcarving	Jeremy Williams
Turning Wooden Toys	Terry Lawrence
Designing and Making Wooden Toys	Terry Kelly
Making Board, Peg and Dice Games	Jeff & Jennie Loader
Members' Guide to Marketing	Jack Pigden
Woodworkers' Career and Educational Source Book	GMC Publications

GMC Publications regularly produces new books on a wide range of woodworking and craft subjects, and an increasing number of specialist magazines, all available on subscription:

MAGAZINES

Woodturning   **Businessmatters**   **Woodcarving**

All these books and magazines are available through bookshops and newsagents, or may be ordered by post from the publishers at 166 High Street, Lewes, East Sussex BN7 1XU, telephone (0273) 477374. Credit card orders are accepted. Please write or phone for the latest information.